T   **DATE DUE**   022004

JUN 3 '78			
OCT. 0 4 1986			
JUL 3 0 1998			

333.7   **Doty, Roy**
D   Where are you going with
that energy?   X56168

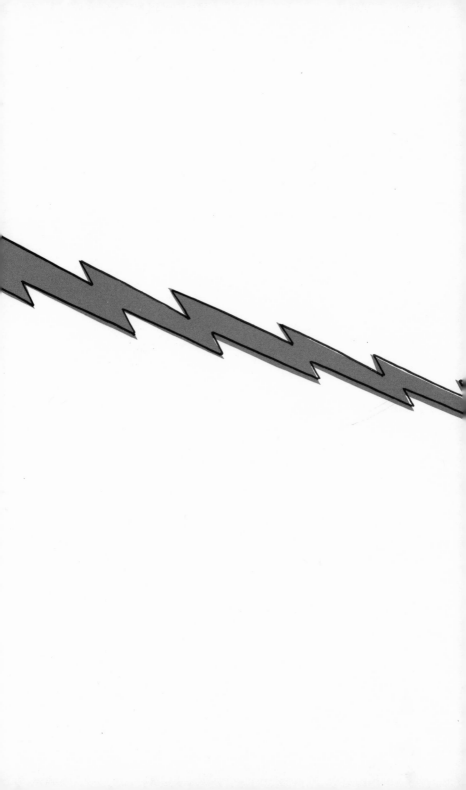

Where are you going with that energy?

Where are you going with that energy?

by Roy Doty
with Leonard Maar

Doubleday & Company, Inc.
Garden City, New York

O22004

Library of Congress Cataloging in Publication Data

Doty, Roy, 1922–
Where are you going with that energy?

Includes index.
1. Power resources—Juvenile literature.
2. Power (Mechanics)—Juvenile literature.
I. Maar, Leonard, joint author.   II. Title.
TJ163.23.D67   333.7
ISBN 0-385-11519-9 Trade
0-385-11520-2 Prebound
Library of Congress Catalog Card Number 75–36587

This book is part of a Museum of Science & Industry/ Chicago series of science books published by Doubleday & Company, Incorporated. The series is designed to inform, stimulate, and challenge youngsters on a wide range of scientific and technological subjects.

Contents

Preface

THE EARLIEST PEOPLE, before they wore clothes or learned to use fire and tools, were among the weakest of animals—yet they survived. Inferior in many ways to the huge, fierce animals with which they competed for food, humans outlived many of them, and over the centuries created civilization as we know it.

Early humans flourished because of two unique qualities that other animals did not develop. People had minds and hands. People discovered energy, which can be simply defined as the capability to do work. For example, killing animals for food with a spear or club meant the hunter had to be close to the beast. That was dangerous. The bow and arrow, the boomerang, and the sling put human and mechanical energy to work giving the hunter the advantage of being able to kill at a distance, thus helping him to survive.

The first people learned to use tools and to harness the forces of nature. They learned how to use the spring in a stick, the weight of a rock. And then they learned to use fire. Fire produces heat, a form of energy that can do work.

Energy has always been available in vast amounts and in many forms. As the years passed and people progressed from the Dark Ages into the present time, their progress was marked by their ability to harness the forces of nature, the resources of the earth, and to put them to work.

This, then, is the story of energy, one of the great mystery stories of all time. What we know about energy today is just a beginning. There is much more to be discovered. There are sources of energy, in almost unlimited quantities, that we have only just begun to understand. You are involved in the energy story for it is unfolding around you every day.

Where are you going with that energy?

FIRE.   The sky darkened as a thunderstorm swept across the jungle. Lightning flashed, struck a tree, and a spark leaped into the dry grass. Fire. How it must have frightened primitive people! But people are the most inventive of all animals, and even though afraid, they felt the fire's heat and saw that it brightened the dark.

In a cold world it is nice to be warm. On a dark night, it is nice to have light. And so fire was brought into the cave. With it came new discoveries, for fire not only gave heat and light, it softened tough food and frightened away animals that hunt by night.

Fire made heat and heat changed things. It made some wood harder. It caused rocks to split. Fire's heat energy could be used as a tool.

The changes heat caused were undoubtedly discovered by accident. One discovery that changed the world probably happened because a rock, called malachite, was near a fire. The rock melted and a golden metal flowed out. We know that metal as copper, man's first metal. Early people shaped copper into tools and ornaments.

For hundreds of years, nobody really understood fire. People thought that it was a kind of matter, like water or air. It wasn't until the late 1700s that chemists figured out that fire is a combining of elements, a chemical process that releases heat. Fire's release of energy, in the form of heat, gave early people a mighty tool.

WATER. Imagine that you are living near a river back in the time of the cave dwellers. A great storm brings heavy rains and the river fills, flooding over its banks. Huge trees are swept away and great boulders moved about. The rushing water has tremendous energy.

Moving water carried the earliest boats and rafts. People could travel and move goods along rivers and streams, and eventually sailors in boats ventured out upon the seas. Early boats took many forms, such as animal skins sewn into bags that would float, reeds tied together, dugout logs, and bark canoes.

When it was understood that water flows downhill, sluices (open pipes), were invented to bring water to

irrigate crops and to wash dirt away in mining.

Water power was the first natural force people harnessed as an extension of their own muscles. Water mills were invented only a few thousand years ago, but they played a very important part in the development of civilization because the mill could do much more work than people could, and it never got tired.

The first water mills consisted of a wheel partly immersed in the flowing stream. The pressure of the water against the vanes of the wheel forced it to turn, rotating the hub to which an axle was attached. The axle, through gears, turned the grinding (or milling) wheel, producing more power than several hundred animals.

WIND. Air is much lighter and less dense than water. The wind isn't constant, as is the flow of a river. Yet people came to realize that moving air would do work. The earliest use of wind power was in helping boats move by sails. The windmill was not developed until much later, probably because of the difficulty in coping with the differences in wind force and direction.

Where does the wind come from? Both wind and water move over our earth because of the sun. Water is evaporated from the sea by the sun's heat and falls back to earth as rain, filling the lakes and rivers. The sun's heat is stored by the earth's surface during the day and rises as the earth cools at night, causing air movement, or wind.

Capturing energy from moving wind or water uses what is called kinetic energy, energy taken from motion. In the case of the windmill, the moving air pushes against the sails (or vanes), turning the wheel to which the sail is attached. As with the water mill, the axle turns and causes work to be done. Windmills are used in many countries of the world and are most often found in coastal areas where the wind is usually stronger and steadier. Land and sea radiate their heat differently, there is more air movement.

We use the energy of the wind principally to power windmills and sailboats. But gliders use this same energy, as do balloons.

ANIMAL POWER. Early in human history, people found that animals could be tamed and made to work. Even in primitive times, warring tribes used prisoners as slaves. The human mind and hand, doing things, improving life, became the restless force that distinguishes man from animal.

The bow and arrow was one of mankind's earliest machines. It used the energy stored in the human body plus the energy released in the spring of the bow through the bowstring to the arrow, which could kill at a distance.

Think of all the animals people have tamed and used to do work. Only a few are shown in our illustration. How many more can you think of? Today, even the dol-

phin works for man in under-sea research. Japanese fishermen still use cormorants (birds), to fish for them.

Humans and animals get their energy from the food they eat. The sun provides the energy to grow the food. We eat even though we are not working; we eat to live. Man power and animal power are really poor ways of getting things done. Living things must rest. Mechanical devices can work on and on and need fuel only when working.

So these were the natural forces available to the early people: muscle power, fire, water, and wind. With this limited knowledge of energy, great cities were built and nations emerged.

COAL. For centuries wood was the main fuel, and it still is in many underdeveloped countries. Coal was first used by the ancient Chinese and other early people. It was found on the surface of the earth but wasn't mined until wood became scarce. Coal was once living plants. Buried under the changing crust of the earth, the plants were compressed, heated, and gradually turned into coal.

Coal is a black rock that burns. It burns with a steady heat that provides an even temperature necessary to melt ore so that copper, iron, and other metals can be obtained. Coal and metalworking go hand in hand.

Coal, when burned, produces heat energy. Heat is needed in many industrial processes, for heat causes

chemical changes. Because they are made from living matter, coal, oil, and wood contain hydrogen and carbon. When these fuels are heated in the presence of oxygen, the elements combine rapidly, causing fire.

There are more than fifteen different kinds of coal. Most important are anthracite, bituminous, and lignite. They are different from each other because of their chemical composition.

Coal can also be changed into gas. Coal gas was used widely before the discovery of and extensive use of petroleum gases. Some coal is found in almost every state in the United States, and in many foreign countries. There are still trillions of tons of coal beneath the land.

STEAM. The story of how people have used energy to do work takes a giant step forward with the invention of the steam engine. When water is heated to the boiling point it vaporizes, changing to steam. The tiny parts of water (its molecules) move faster and faster as they are heated. This expansion creates pressure and becomes kinetic energy.

Water power, wind power, animal power—all are less powerful than steam power. Steam engines can do much more work, more quickly and less expensively. Once the inventor James Watt had built his steam engine to pump water from the mines of England in 1763, steam engines were put to work to do hundreds of jobs such as pulling

trains, powering boats, running factories—even running cars and buses. The first elevator was steam powered.

The steam engine has been called the greatest single invention of all time. People now had the ability to use the energy in heat as power. When we think of what this means in terms of bettering the way of life for the world's people, it is, indeed, a giant step. In other words, more goods and services were made available to more people.

Each person in the United States today has as much power to use as that which could be produced by one hundred slaves. Because we have learned to change energy into useful power, we have the highest standard of living ever known.

ANIMAL OILS. It seems strange that even while the steam engine was being invented and perfected, as coal was coming into use as the major fuel, whale oil was still the source of illumination in many homes in the Western world. Walrus, seals, and some fish were also caught for the oil that could be rendered from their fat.

On the other hand, it is not so strange, considering how people have generally taken the most readily available energy without regard for the consequences. Millions of whales have been killed since people learned that the whale oil burned brightly and made an excellent, fine lubricant. Whales are still considered of great value, and thousands are caught each year.

Whale oil was used for illumination well into the 1700s. It was only when whales became scarce that alternate sources of lighting were sought. Coal gas was the most readily available substitute—cheaper and easier to produce. Later, kerosene was used. But it is significant to know that we used whale oil because we wanted light.

Other animals provide heat and light for people living in remote parts of the world. The Eskimos use seal oil and some fish oil. Fat from these animals is cooked (rendered), releasing the oil. In those parts of our world where there is no wood or coal, where people rely on hunting and fishing for food and fuel, using all of the animal makes sense.

PETROLEUM. For centuries people had known about places where oil leaked out on the surface of the land. Noah used pitch to make the ark watertight, and the Romans used it to lubricate the wheels of their chariots. The early Chinese drilled the first oil wells using bamboo pipes and brass bits.

With whale oil growing scarce, and coal gas expensive and complicated to produce, a search for a new illuminating oil began. In 1859 Colonel E. A. Drake drilled the first oil well in North America at Titusville, Pennsylvania.

Petroleum, like coal, is a fossil fuel, formed in much the same way as coal. The petroleum trapped within the earth is a huge source of potential energy. At about the

same time that oil wells were first drilled in America, the internal-combustion engine was being perfected. This made the automobile possible, and later the airplane.

When petroleum is refined, it can be broken up into many different parts—kerosene, jet fuel, gasoline, diesel fuel, and literally thousands of other by-products. And so a tremendous industry came into being as the search for and production of petroleum grew.

We don't know for certain just how much petroleum is buried in the earth. We do know that someday we will have used it all up. The same is true of natural gas, yet we use more of these two sources of energy than all others combined.

ELECTRICITY. We have been reading about the natural sources of energy that people learned to use as civilization developed. In the eighteenth century, people began studying two closely related, invisible forms of energy— electricity and magnetism. In the nineteenth century, these studies were applied to the generation and supply of electricity to homes and factories.

You cannot touch electricity, or see it. We can only describe it because of what it does. A current of electricity flowing through a wire is a means of transferring energy from the source—the power plant—to your home.

The study of electricity led to the invention of the telegraph, radio and television, radar, and the discovery of

What hath God wrought

atomic energy. We take electricity for granted because it is always available to us.

The first power plants were designed by Thomas Edison. They were coal-fueled, steam generators. The first three began making electricity in 1882. Two of them were in England and one in New York City.

In places where there are swift rivers, dams are built and the falling water runs generators producing electricity. This is called hydroelectric power. In many cities, oil is used as the fuel to heat the water that makes the steam that provides the energy to generate electricity. Atomic energy is also used to fuel steam-generating electric power plants.

The cave dwellers captured fire to give them light and heat. Imagine what those early people would think if they came into our homes today. We flick a switch and the lights go on, we turn a dial and see pictures that may come from the other side of the world.

Of course, electricity does much more. It runs factories, steel- and paper-making machinery, and machines that make our clothes. It runs trains and subways, radio and television stations, school and hospital equipment, food processing and freezing plants, and it powered the presses that printed this book. Electricity has become a part of our way of life—something we take for granted and could not do without.

All across the United States there are hundreds of power plants generating electricity to meet the great demand for this clean, useful form of energy. Within the next few years all of these stations will be joined in a single network so that a sudden need in any part of the country can be filled from a power plant across the nation, eliminating the possibility of blackouts which have occurred in some cities during times of peak demand. Indeed, we live in the electric age.

Looking at the wonderful benefits of electricity, it would seem that we have just about solved our energy problems. What more could we want? But now, we have to take into consideration what all this progress costs.

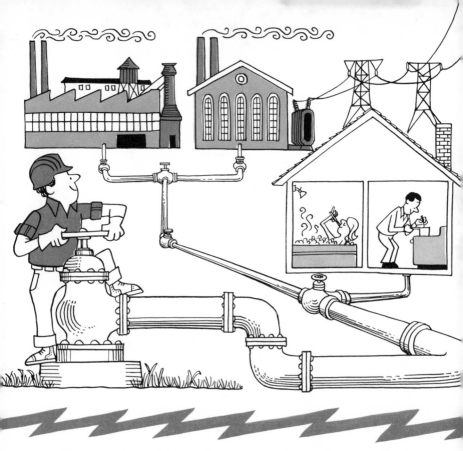

NATURAL GAS. Great quantities of natural gas are stored in reservoirs in the earth. Where some leaked out of the ground, ancient fire worshippers used these gas leaks as a source for their eternal flames. Like coal and oil, natural gas was formed as living matter buried beneath the earth decayed and was subjected to great heat and pressure.

Wells are drilled to tap the reservoirs of natural gas. The gas is carried through thousands of miles of pipelines across the country and is used in 40 million homes for heating and cooking. Natural gas can be liquified and transported in truck or by ship, and like petroleum, it can be refined and made into many products.

EXPLOSIVES. In seeking to solve the mystery of natural forces, someone, centuries ago in China, learned about the explosive quality of gunpowder. This brought about the use of guns and blew the armored knight into history. Cannon and rifles changed warfare when people made weapons that could kill at great distances.

But explosives, such as dynamite or TNT, can be used to good purpose in mining and construction.

Explosions release great amounts of energy, and this form of power has been a center of study and fascination for centuries. It was through experimentation with explosive gases that the internal-combustion engine came about.

THE INTERNAL-COMBUSTION ENGINE is not an energy source, but it is vitally important to the energy story because it is one of the largest consumers of energy. These engines have made transportation available to millions of people. One fourth of all the energy used in the United States is for transportation, and 60 per cent of that amount is gasoline.

The first engine designed so that fuel burned inside the cylinder was a gunpowder engine built in 1673. The lack of a more suitable fuel held back further developments until the early 1800s. A number of engines were invented then which used coal gas as fuel.

As petroleum became available, two main types of en-

gines were perfected—the gasoline engine developed by Gottlieb Daimler, and the diesel engine of Rudolf Diesel. Modern versions of these engines power most of today's cars, trucks, planes, and power tools.

The airplane, with an internal-combustion piston engine spinning a propeller, is limited to an air speed of about 450 miles per hour. With the invention of the gas turbine, the jet engine became possible, boosting air speed to well over 1,000 miles per hour.

People can now travel almost anywhere at tremendous speeds. But once again, we must look at the cost. We are using up the world's supply of petroleum at an ever-increasing rate. What can we do about it?

HIGH-ENERGY FUELS. The discovery of gunpowder led to the invention of the rocket. The Chinese, in their battles with the invading Mongols in A.D. 1200, attached small rockets to their arrows.

Gunpowder-fueled rockets have been used in wars ever since. During the War of 1812, the British used them against Fort McHenry, moving Francis Scott Key to write about "the rocket's red glare" in our national anthem.

Robert H. Goddard is considered the father of modern rockets. In 1926 he sent up the first liquid-propellant rocket, and although his work was considered too dangerous by many, he continued to experiment and made great contributions to rocketry.

Rockets depend on fuels that release a great deal of energy to provide the thrust that speeds them on their flight. Many such fuels have been developed, both solid and liquid. The solids are combinations of materials that burn intensely when ignited. Rockets using solids are the simplest in construction, fast to ignite and stable in performance.

Liquid-propellant rockets are more complex but produce more thrust. The Saturn 5 rocket that powered Apollo II to the moon developed 7.5 million pounds of thrust. There are many combinations of chemicals used to fuel liquid-propellant rockets, such as liquid oxygen, and a kerosenelike hydrocarbon.

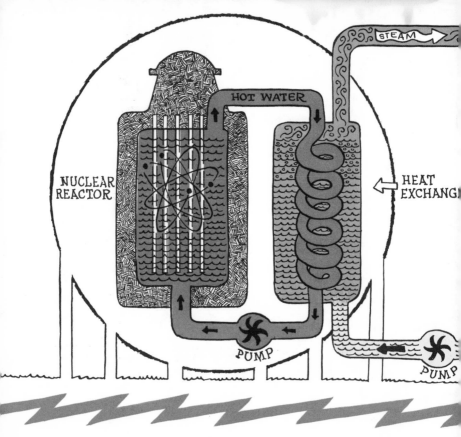

ENERGY FROM THE ATOM. For more than two thousand years it was believed that the atom was the smallest particle of matter. Late in the 1800s, scientists began to suspect that this was not true, and through the work of many, it was soon learned that the atom could be split and heat energy resulted.

This splitting of atoms can be controlled so that the heat energy boils water to make the steam that turns a turbine. The turbine runs a generator, making electricity. Today, millions of homes use electricity generated in this way.

The fuel for the atomic-energy plant is uranium, a highly concentrated source of energy. One pound of ura-

nium used to make electricity is equal to 2,000 tons of coal. But we must remember that uranium is mined, and there is just so much of it in the earth's crust. Some day, it too will be used up.

And there are other problems as well. Atomic-energy plants produce dangerously radioactive waste. How this waste is disposed of is a major concern, for it will remain dangerous for thousands of years. In the past few years, the cost of building atomic-energy plants has increased considerably.

If these problems can be solved, the energy of the atom will certainly help meet the increasing demand for energy in a world with an ever-increasing number of people.

SOLAR ENERGY. The sun is the source of almost all the energy we use. The sun's heat gave life to the plants and creatures that died centuries ago and are now coal and oil. The sun's heat makes our weather, causing the rains that make our fresh water, and the winds. The sun is our energy center.

Look at the solar-heated home above. The sun's heat is collected by panels on the roof containing tubing filled with water. The sun-heated water is stored in a bank of rocks which hold the heat until it is needed. Imagine farms of such heat collectors circulating hot water or gas, heated by the sun, to drive an electric power plant. Solar-energy centers are being planned.

40

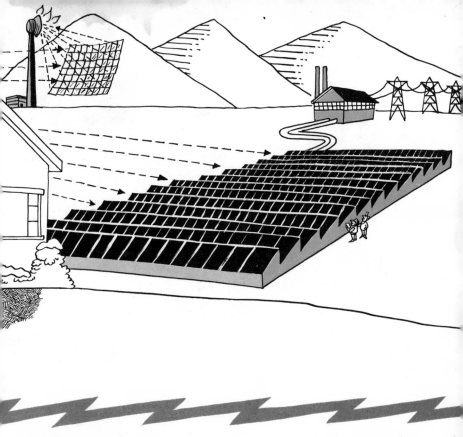

The heat from the sun is an almost unlimited source of energy. Our government, and many companies, are spending millions of dollars to find ways to use solar energy.

The heat from the sun can be captured through solar cells which turn the heat into electricity. Solar cells powered the Skylab which supported nine astronauts for 171 days in orbit around the earth. Solar cells are expensive to make, so many people are studying them to find cheaper methods of manufacture.

There are many other plans to use the clean, abundant energy from the sun as a major source of power. Just as the sun has made life on our planet possible, it may prove to be the best source of energy for the future.

GEOTHERMAL ENERGY. The inside of the earth is very hot. Heat is energy. Geothermal means earth heat energy. The problem is bringing this energy source to the surface and putting it to use.

Where steam is trapped under the earth, a hole can be drilled, releasing the steam into pipes for use in a power plant to produce electricity. There aren't many of these dry-steam reservoirs, but there are two other kinds of geothermal energy—hot water and dry-rock deposits.

The hot water found within the earth is often corrosive, eating pipes and damaging equipment such as pumps. Systems have to be developed so that this difficult-to-handle hot water can be put to work.

Hot, dry volcanic rock under the earth is another energy source. Its heat energy can be used by drilling a hole into the hot rock and pumping in water. A second hole allows the hot water to return to the surface where it turns to steam. Such an experiment has already been done, proving that this method will work. We now know that we can tap the heat energy inside the earth.

There is still much to be learned about the hot insides of the earth. Scientists are working on a project to drill deep holes into the molten rock chambers thousands of feet down. They hope to learn what the earth's hot center contains, how it affects the surface, and how its great heat energy can be used.

ENERGY FROM THE OCEANS. Much of the surface of our world is covered by the oceans. These huge bodies of water contain energy in almost unlimited amounts. Scientists are seeking ways to use the oceans' energy to generate electricity.

The power of the tides in some places is tremendous. In France and in the Soviet Union, power plants have been built that use the rise and fall of the tides to spin turbines attached to generators that make electricity. There are a number of other places in our world where tidal power could be used.

Over the flat surface of the oceans, the winds blow strong and more steadily than on land. Scientists are ex-

perimenting with very large windmills with vanes like egg beaters. These windmills will make electricity that can be used to extract hydrogen from the sea water. Hydrogen is a clean-burning fuel. Many experts think that hydrogen will someday replace gasoline and oil. There are already hydrogen-fueled automobiles being tested.

The surface of the ocean is heated by the sun creating a layer of warm water. Beneath the surface the water is much cooler. The difference in temperature could yield energy. Even the ocean currents, such as the Gulf Stream, are being studied to see how their flow can be used as energy. These are but a few of the plans to get energy from the oceans.

CRUSHED SHALE

VAPOR-COLLECT TUBES

GAS BURNER

BURNED SHALE

OIL SHALES AND SANDS. Spread over 11 million acres of Colorado, Utah, and Wyoming, an estimated 600 million barrels of oil are trapped in rocks called shale. Another 600 million barrels of oil are thought to be trapped in the Athabasca tar sands in Canada. That's a great deal of oil, and if it can be recovered, it would add a lot to our energy supply.

A number of companies, with government help, are working to solve the problems involved in freeing the oil from the shale and sand. So far, efforts have been disappointing.

What are the problems? First of all, the shale rocks have to be crushed and heated to release the oil. Ten tons

GAS

GAS

OIL →

of rock are needed to produce one ton of oil. The left-
over rock, thousands and thousands of tons, has to be put
somewhere. Large amounts of water are needed in the re-
covery process. Water is scarce in that part of the country. Then, the oil has to be refined, a costly process. Huge
oil plants will change the ecology of that wild country.

Getting the oil out of the tar sands is proving to be just
as difficult. The sand is hard and sharp. It wrecks the
digging machinery. In the winter it is as hard as rock,
and in the summer it turns soft and gooey. Oil from tar
sands also has to be refined, and the costs are very high.

The promise of oil from these abundant reservoirs
hasn't come true. But new methods are being tried.

FUEL CELLS AND BATTERIES. A fuel cell is a source of electricity generated through direct conversion of the energy released by combining gases, such as hydrogen and oxygen, in an electrochemical reaction. Although the first fuel cell was demonstrated in 1839 by Sir William Grove, nothing much was done to develop fuel cells.

Making electricity from a continuous chemical reaction is a very efficient process requiring very little fuel. Fuel cells have other advantages—they have no moving parts, they don't make noise, they don't cause extensive air pollution, and they can be carried about. Fuel cells provided electric power for the Apollo and other spacecraft. Cars and trucks can use fuel cells instead of gasoline or diesel

oil. Homes have been experimentally electrified by fuel cells using 30 to 40 per cent less fuel than a conventionally fueled and powered home.

Batteries store electricity, but eventually they have to be replaced—as in a flashlight—or recharged—as does your car battery. Here, too, as interest in energy has increased, new kinds of batteries that provide a stronger electric current for a longer period of time are being developed. One new type of lead-acid battery won't leak, can be left on the shelf for over a year between uses, and is not too expensive. These new batteries are being used to power portable tools such as drills, grass clippers, razors, and high-power lights.

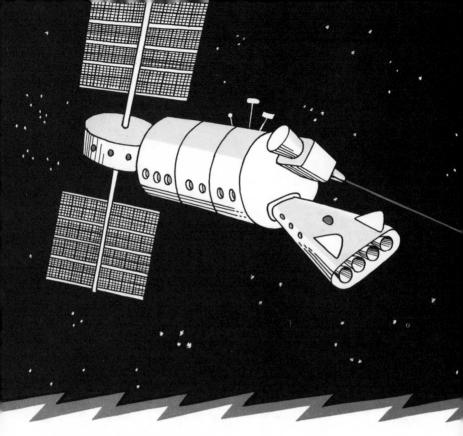

DIRECT CONVERSION. The fuel cell and the solar cell convert energy directly into electricity. They are valuable because they do not require an engine to put the energy to work as does a car fueled by gasoline, or a power plant fueled by oil or natural gas. They do not make noise and they minimize pollution. They have no moving parts and they are portable.

In the illustration above, two space stations are sending the sun's energy down to earth. On the left, solar cells use the sun's heat to power a laser beam which, in turn, carries energy down to an earth station where it is converted into electricity.

On the right is a satellite with solar panels covered

with wings more than five miles square. In orbit, more than 200,000 miles above the earth, a single solar power station could supply half of the electricity needed by New York City. The electricity generated by the panels would be sent down to earth as microwaves and converted to electricity by a receiving station. One group of scientists think that a space colony should be established on which thousands of people would live while they are building a number of solar power stations. This is a very costly project, but it could solve our energy problems for centuries.

Direct conversion of energy to electricity solves the problems of energy shortage and of pollution. Maybe the cost of power stations in space isn't too high after all.

WHAT ABOUT THE FUTURE? Because there is only so much coal, natural gas, and petroleum to be found in the earth, we know that someday they will be used up. We don't have to be afraid of running out of energy if we use our present resources wisely while we develop new energy sources. We are beginning to realize that energy is one of our greatest treasures.

In this book we have touched on only some of the ways being explored to replace the fuels that are becoming scarce. Based on the best expert guesses, petroleum will last for less than one hundred years. Coal reserves could carry us through another two or three hundred years, and because it can be made into liquid fuels, it could fill our needs. Growing special green plants on land or in the ocean, and processing them into gas, which, in turn, can be made into liquid fuel, is another alternative. And we have read about many other alternatives that are being developed.

But we must use energy more wisely. Each of us can help. Remind the drivers in your family to stay under the

55-miles-per-hour national speed limit. Urge your family to combine automobile trips so that your car is used efficiently. Turn off lights and appliances when they are not needed. Talk with your parents about lowering the setting of your thermostat to 68 degrees and raising the air conditioner setting, to 70 degrees. Could your home be better insulated? You will need less heat and cooling if it is.

Most of the electricity we use is generated from burning petroleum and coal to make steam to power turbines that spin generators. Saving electricity means that we will burn less fossil fuel. Scientists are searching for alternate ways to generate electricity. No reasonable method can be ignored. One suggestion is to fly great kitelike sails out over the ocean. The energy of the wind would be converted to electricity that would be sent back down to earth through cables. These energy sails would be brought down when the winds are light. It sounds almost impossible, but some people think it will work. Shouldn't we try it?

In the United States, with only one sixth of the world's population, we use one third of the world's energy. We waste more than 30 per cent through heat loss and other causes. And most of the ways we generate power cause pollution. Because we have had cheap and abundant energy, we have used it wastefully. We cannot afford to do that any longer. There are many people in other parts of the world who are not as energy rich as we.

HERE ARE some things to think about. There is a tribe of people living on an island in the Pacific Ocean who never let their fires go out because they have never learned how to make fire. In rural India, dried animal manure is still a main source of fuel for cooking fires. In Venezuela in South America, one of the world's oil-rich countries, many of the people outside the large cities have only charcoal as fuel. In Africa, families still gather sticks for their cooking fires. In Thailand, 97 per cent of the people are dependent on firewood as their only fuel.

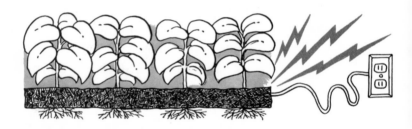

The energy shortage is a life-and-death problem for many of the world's people.

Even if we try not to waste things, there is still rubbish to be gotten rid of. But even rubbish is valuable as an energy source. Many cities are processing garbage to reclaim valuable metals and paper. The remaining trash can be processed and turned into a usable fuel. Even our trash contains potential energy.

Saving energy isn't a job for just a few of us. Many large companies that use vast amounts of energy are working to use less. Our government is deeply involved in energy-saving programs. Saving energy must become everybody's job. Talk with your family and your teachers

about energy-saving projects. You and your friends can help. Working together we can become energy savers, not energy wasters.

The mystery of energy is slowly being solved. Today, we know much more about it than we did twenty years ago. Tomorrow, we will know more, for we have only just begun to explore new sources and methods of bringing energy supplies to more people to improve their lives. Through saving energy by using it more wisely, we will gain the time we need to develop and change over to new, less polluting sources.

There is still so much to learn about energy. It is one of the most interesting studies for it is the story of peoples' progress through time. Perhaps, someday, if you are interested, you will be working on one of the projects you have been reading about.

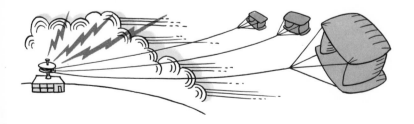

Index

20–21; hydrogen and carbon in, 21; and industrial processes, 20–21; kinds, 21; and metalworking, 20; what it is, 20

Coal gas, 21, 25, 26, 34

Construction, use of explosives in, 33

Copper, 13, 20; coal and, 20; early use of, 13

Cormorants, 19

Currents, ocean, energy from, 45. *See also* Tidal power; Water power

Daimler, Gottlieb, 35

Dams, and electricity, 29

Diesel, Rudolf, 35

Diesel fuel, 27, 35, 48–49

Dolphins, 18–19

Drake, Colonel E. A., 26

Dry-rock geothermal energy, 42, 43

Dynamite, 33

Earth heat (geothermal) energy, 42–43

Edison, Thomas A., 29

Electricity, 28–31; atomic energy and uranium and, 38–39; conservation of, 52–53; direct conversion into, 50–51; fuel cells and batteries, 48–49, 50; geothermal energy and, 42; and ocean's energy, 44–45; power plants, 29, 31, 38–39, 42, 53; solar cells and, 41, 50–51; uses of, 28–29,

30–31; wind power and, 44–45, 53

Elevator, first, steam power and, 23

Energy (power), 9–10; animal (muscle), 18–19; animal oils, 24–25; atomic, 29, 38–39; coal, 20–21 (*see also* Coal); conservation of, 52–53, 54–55; defined, 9; direct conversion into electricity, 50–51; electric, 28–31, 50–51 (*see also* Electricity); explosives and, 33, 34–35; fire and heat and, 9, 12–13 (*see also* Fire; Heat); fuel cells and batteries, 48–49; geothermal, 42–43; high-energy fuels and, 36–37; hydroelectric, 29; and internal-combustion engines, 33, 34–35; kinetic, 17, 22; natural gas, 27, 32; oceans and, 44–45; oil shales and sands, 46–47; petroleum, 26–27 (*see also* Petroleum); and pollution, 50, 51, 53, 55; from rubbish (garbage), 54; solar, 40–41, 50–51; steam, 22–23 (*see also* Steam power); water, 14–15, 29, 44–45; wind, 16–17, 44–45, 53

Engines. *See* Internal-combustion engines

England, first use of steam engines in, 22–23

Eskimos, and use of seal and fish oil, 25

Explosives, 33; and high-energy

Temperature differences, ocean water, energy from, 45

Thailand, firewood as a source of fuel in, 54

Thermostat settings, energy conservation and, 53

Tidal power, 44

Titusville, Pa., first oil well drilled at (1859), 26

TNT, 33

Tools, power, 35; new type of lead-acid batteries and, 49

Trains: electric, 30; steam, 23

Trash, energy from, 54

Travel (transportation): electricity and, 30; internal-combustion engines and, 34–35; petroleum and, 34, 35; steam and, 22–23, water power and, 14

Truck engines, 35

Turbines, electric, 53; tidal power and, 44

Uranium, as fuel for atomic-energy plants, 38–39

Venezuela, use of charcoal as fuel in, 54

Walruses, oil from, 24

War of 1812, use of gunpowder-fueled rockets in, 36

Water evaporation, and wind power, 16

Water mills, 15; first, 15

Water power, 14–15, 17; energy from the oceans and, 44–45; and hydroelectric power, 29; and irrigation, 14; and mills, 15, 17; and mining, 15; and steam power, 22–23; and travel, 14

Watt, James, 22

Weapons (warfare), 33, 36

Whale oil, 24–25, 26

Windmills, 16, 17, 45

Wind power, 16–17; and electricity, 44–45, 53; and windmills, 16, 17, 45

Wood, 21; as fuel, 21, 54; hydrogen and carbon in, 21; replaced by coal, 20, 21

Roy Doty is a nationally known free-lance artist whose work regularly appears in numerous major publications such as *Newsweek, Business Week* and the New York *Times*. He is familiar to *Popular Science* readers as author-cartoonist of the monthly "Wordless Workshop," and his "Laugh-In" newspaper comic strip was nationally syndicated. An inventor and do-it-yourselfer hobbyist, Mr. Doty is the creator of the Popular Science Picture Clock Kit. He lives in Connecticut with his authoress wife and four children in one of the world's few solar-heated homes, which he helped design.

Leonard Maar is a professional writer who works in communication and advertising. He has written for numerous national magazines and, with his wife, is the author of a cookbook. The Maars live on the Connecticut shore with their two children, three cats, and two dogs.

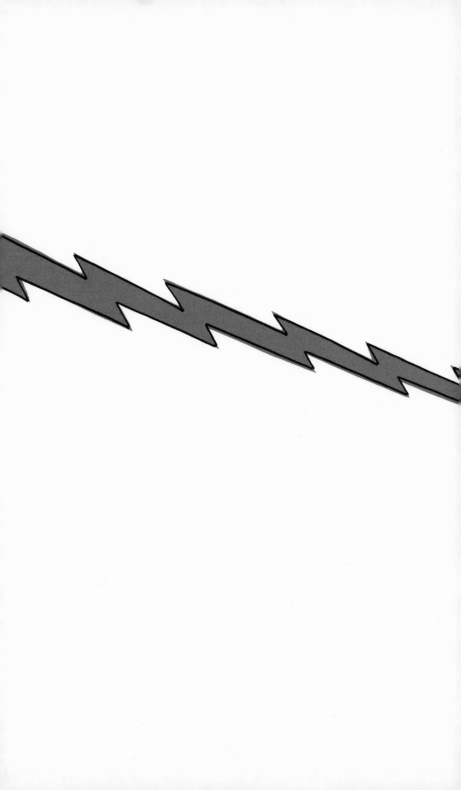